But Never This

B. Sue Stephenson

Cover painting by Prasanna

Forward

With all the energies of its
potential gathered together
-this moment-
quivering with impending manifestation,
Life at its most intense aliveness.

Imagine that you are invited
to be present,
to be a witness of the moment
when Life sprouts as "This".

This poet needs no invitation.
She lives there
where "This" is not "This" yet
-the juncture-
where Life blossoms as "This".
For the poet, every "This" is a whisper,
an announcement of Life's aliveness,
but

-Never This-

                                        -Prasanna,
May 2024

TRUTH

Truth sits on the laps of statues in the park.
It stops the clock on the train station wall
And blows the white aprons of maids
   in a row.

It has no siblings,
No fortune or pockets:
Only feet hollow and still.

Truth lies at the bottom of time.
It hails no one, remaining silent
When the innocent are accused
Or the boat leaves its mooring.

Truth is the place between raindrops.
It informs death and its opposite, air.

Truth will leave your hat alone.
Your plans will stand.
Your heart will see.
Your hands will know.

BUTTERMILK SKY

Dividing beyond and here,
This buttermilk sky sets your day,
Informs your heart of ceiling,
Reflects pieces of your life here.

It shows them to God on the other side
Who would be you specifically
    if he could,
To view the underneath,
Feel sweet sorrow in his heart,
The rain on his skin.

TIME AND WIND

It turns out
That time and wind are really the same.
You flail or sway in them
   without choice,
And whatever breaks your trunk or limb
Or leans you so long you grow that way
Also defines you.
You notice you have changed.
You look around
Expecting to see the reason
And there is nothing.

ABSOLUTE

Our souls are not together,
We did not really meet.
Our bodies are only
Confessions of one god's passion,
And our minds mere curios
Within the great oneness.

But we don our separateness
  in the morning,
Kiss the other,
Make his tea.
We play as children
Under the card table tent
With babes and houses
And soldiers and wounds,
Pretending the vastness doesn't exist.

And sometimes,
When we tire of the game by nightfall
The absolute rushes in
Like water:
Soaks the prayer,
The mantra,
The dream,
The eyes of lovers.

THIS BIRD

This bird does not exist.
It's only a manifestation of passion
Built within a wing,
Folding upon itself,
Creating another wing
And the imperative
To love the wind,
Which only blows
Because there are wings
And craving,
Forward and back in time.

MID-WINTER

Like an inhalation halted at its extreme,
Winter waits in the nadir of time,
The silence of dreams.

Only buds know the truth:

Sadness lies deep like a sunken boat.
Renewal is fragile.
Patience is action.
All is not lost.

THE WINDOW

Self opens its window-eyes
To human weather and sun of place.

Human takes the window to heart,
Opens his eyes too
And gazes out
As morning dew-ness and queries
Mingle in his hands.

All looking looks back
And because of the window
   and its edges
Each looker sees more than there is
   to know.
This makes the human a dream
And causes the self
To sleep with the window open.

THE PAST

Water,
Movement.

The past is transparent.

In it are tumbling pebbles and boulders,
Fish jumping toward the present
  to spawn.

LIGHT

Darkness cries tears of light.
Grief has crystals within it.

They sustain us.

Light is friends with all dark lakes.

It does not come from darkness,
Or itself, light,
Or from something
Or from nothing.

It is the paper around the gift,
It is the inevitable thief of differences.

go to the garden

walk upon petals of dreams

fallen in the night

NIGHT

There are so many shades of black.
Death must be like that:
Dark mountain behind darker
   stand of tall trees,
Barely discernable fields mid-distance,
Deep sky.
Though you can only see these
   things with your soul
Which is part of the darkness anyway,
Wanting to be with the trees
   most intimately,
And know everything else
As if existence depended on it.

WATCHING

Watching the birds,
Considering the weather,
Wondering when the big opening
    will come.

Anticipating delight
    is delightful.

Everything is about to happen.

UNION

Come from your sky,
Cold before the touch,
Before the kiss.

Faith into the slot
Where only your being may enter.

No one can describe to you
Before your fall
The reflection you will become,
The song that will sing you.

You will be prayer on the water,
Joy in blood,
Green in the red wine,
Evening desert sky in a white teacup,
Birds who love,
Light making love in the dark
Begetting more light.

And when your joy
Comes to rest at your own feet
There will be no country
No sun
No sea
No way
No death
No explanation.

BEAUTY

This beauty here
Makes me lie down,
Stop breathing,
Listen to the crickets,
And find that I am nothing.

PAINT BY AWARENESS

This two-dimensional moment
  has everything:
Covered bridge and autumn leaves,
Creek water with white ripples,
Peaceful blue pond with ducks and reeds,
Brush strokes just so.

I no longer have the box
But the brushes are still soft
And the little containers are still here
  on my desk.

Between the seen and the known
There are still a few small, numbered
  spaces of nothingness,
So I can see God,
Though one of the ducks might fly away
Through any of these uncertainties.

BETWEEN STORMS

Winter takes a breath
In the stillness before wind.
Water settles down the leaves.
Time moves cautiously,
Grateful for the old kind of life:
Brief,
Unmastered,
Innocent.

OPEN

Open the door
Let it snow in here

Our love has nothing to do
with the weather.

I AM THE ROSE

The rose is here,
Within.

It cares not about your opinion,
How you place it in your life.

It only cares about the bees
That fly between us
Landing in our yellow centers,
Stripes wiggling,
Legs moving,
Buzzing.

DARKNESS IS

Darkness is longing for winter,
For death among the lively and joyful,
For the place where earth is
  only rock,
  only black heat,
For the still nothing at the edge of
  experience
Where creation is confused
 And must come up with
  a new plan,
  a new paradox,
Yet another love.

SPLASH

Existence splashed
Into the summer pond.
The bears were astonished
To find themselves there
With angry crows
Lovely deer
And the fish.

BORROWED

First spring morning
stirs the moments
you have packed away carefully
in your head and heart.

Confused and aroused,
you are changed now.
Birds carry your sentences
with them in their beaks for their nest,
and peach blossoms strike you down
on your way out the door.

Air and breeze and sun are one,
and you no longer borrow your breath
from winter.

Everything and everyone is asking,
"Who am I",
already knowing the answer.

SWEET

sweet apple to dirt

after rain and time and sun

dirt to apple sweet

EXISTENCE

Golden morning light on white petals.
Shadows between.

Clusters of old insides and outsides,
Remains of roses past.

All are buffeted by the dry autumn wind.

Existence has always existed,
But never this.

GREEN

The possibility of green
Could not have been described
Before new leaves appeared,
Enticing me out of here
To the where leaves meet oceans,
Waves meet angels,
And manifestation is simultaneous
And synonymous
With dying.

PEACE

This sleep is darker,
More moist,
As if having fallen through years
    of autumn leaves,
As if having settled
In the land of the deepest self
Who has ceased wanting
And stopped asking "Why?",
Which has left the air there empty
    of sound
So the dreamer may awaken
And dance.

AUTUMN

Days are shorter
And there is one red leaf
On the maple tree.

Light entering our eyes is more golden,
And love is held closer to the heart.

I want nothing.
Existence is joy itself.

And as sunflowers bow their heads
I hear the birds talking
About things I don't understand.

FLOWER

Inside the curve of one petal
  is a secret.
If you go there you must leave
  your self behind,
Slide into its subtle shadows,
The translucence there:
Be the eye of the bee
And the laugh of God,
Intimately known
To each other.

SADNESS

You have to keep sadness around,
Even if it's just a fine dust
Resting on your life,
Even if it's only a thin darkness
    underlying your afternoon,
A bunch of crows,
Or tiny hesitations in your step.

It will inform everything,
And keep you from drifting away.

AUTUMN ROSE

Autumn rose lays its petals
  like eyelids
On the last evening light,
On the back of sorrow's delicate hands.
It gathers the huge and powerful irony
  of my tiny life
And places it upon.

Amber hush comes,
Wanting the blossom and the hour both,

And because I cannot swim
We fall between the walls of time
Where survival is insignificant
And only this rose knows my name.

CLOUDS

Clouds are here
  because of rivers
Which are here
  because of mountains and hills
And because there is variation
In color and shadow and song.

Time spreads them all thin
So we may see.

IN THE WIND

In the wind
Leaves become infinite,
And birds are only spaces in the blue sky
Where desire might have been.

Their union is known only to time,
Which rests on the bottom of the world,
Waiting.

BRAHMAN

Our love is one,
Though I do not exist,
And I don't know about you.

Whatever is center blossoms like the
  lotus flower,
Roots in the darkest muck,
Head above water,
Petals open to our sun
And the suns of others.

What flower isn't the only one,
The only existence?

LAST NIGHT

Last night
I went to bed,
But my sleep was stolen by the sky.

Clouds changed on and on.
Moon, usually so constant,
Allowed her subtle light to become
    caught in the shifting,
Making my life tiny and narrow
Against too many shades to understand,
And the crisp silhouette of the pine
By the creek.

Made in the USA
Las Vegas, NV
26 December 2024

15317926R00069